HER MOTHER'S EYES

Also by David Brazier

A Guide to Psychodrama

Beyond Carl Rogers:
Towards a Psychotherapy for the 21st Century

Zen Therapy

The Feeling Buddha

The New Buddhism

Who Loves Dies Well

Love and Its Disappointment:
The Meaning of Life, Therapy and Art

David Brazier

http://amidatrust.typepad.com/dharmavidya
http://www.facebook.com/pages/David-Brazier/79513078219
http://www.facebook.com/groups/132066556872260/Brazier/79513078219
http://twitter.com/#!/dharmavidya
http://amidatrust.ning.com

HER MOTHER'S EYES

And Other Poems

DAVID BRAZIER

QUG Publishing

To Kaspa and Fiona
and their cultivation of the written word

QUG Publishing
Published by the Quaker Universalist Group.
www.qug.org.uk

Cover design by Richard Crookes from an untitled work in acrylic on canvas by E. Dickie, 2009.

ISBN 978-0-948232-28-2

CONTENTS

PREFACE

I never had any great expectation of my poetry being published so it was not written with publication in mind. Nonetheless, it is good to see this collection now appearing in print.

My approach to writing poetry is an eclectic one and as such my poems are not likely to fit into a niche poetry magazine. The poems in this collection are written in many different styles, though people tell me there is a recognisable "voice" running through this multiplicity. It is not easy to assess one's own work. Sometimes I write more in a spirit of inspiration and at other times of experimentation. There are times when I wake in the middle of the night with a fully formed sonnet in my head; there are other times when I play around with words out of a simple fascination with language. Poetry has a multi-layered quality. The content may be important, but so are what the poem says about language and the variation it gives upon the rhyme and rhythm of life.

Often my style is influenced by the work of other poets, but there is usually also an element of irony or turn of meaning. T.S.Eliot spoke about how all writing comes out of a tradition yet every piece of writing subtly changes that tradition, not just by addition, but by changing the manner in which the whole tradition will be viewed thereafter. Of course, a single work has only limited influence, but each is an expression not just of something personal but also of a collective need. I am sure that my urge to write, like that of all who do so, does not spring from purely personal considerations. It is a response, and therefore a contribution, to a tradition and that tradition has a great many inter-related facets. Different poems address different aspects. At the same time, it cannot be said that one is conscious of all this when writing. In fact, in order to write a special kind of unconsciousness has to prevail. One has to be in a kind of trance in order to produce and in that trance one both opens to something beyond oneself and also becomes blind to what one is doing. Subjectively, at the time, I am simply responding to something I have seen, or heard, or read, or thought, and some music of words starts to play.

It is all my mother's fault, really. My mother, Irene, was a great lover of poetry and I was brought up on it. She liked Kipling and other poets who wrote about the spirit of Englishness. This, of course, is not something that has been in fashion in recent years, but it still influences me. She gave me a love of England, the English countryside, traditional values and the English language. When I was only nine my mother gave me an etymological dictionary and it became one of my favourite books. I would pore over the meanings of words and their relation to one another. She also liked me to learn poems by heart and recite them to her, so I got used to the form and flow of sounds and rhythm, though I only ever studied these things as formal subjects in English Literature at school – the one subject that I failed.

I am fascinated by poetic form and by the arguments poets have about what constitutes poetry. My approach is a broad and inclusive one, both with respect to form and content, as is evident from the many types of verse included in this collection. A lot of my writing is experimental, driven as much by curiosity as purpose, seeking out the possible within the play of meanings. In one sense, it is the *Nonsense* poems that exhibit the under-lying spirit of all the others.

There are many situations and influences that can lead me to write a poem. I can be triggered into writing by something I have seen or a story in the news that has touched me in some way. The *Society* poems, including the title poem *Her Mother's Eyes,* which was written in response to what I heard when I was in Bosnia just after the civil war, are of this type. Or the poem can be triggered by an event in my own life, as those in the *Who am I?* section. And, like many poets, I find that poetry may best express some of my thoughts and feelings about the great intangibles, such as those poems included in the *Love, Nature* and *Philosophy* sections. One of the commonest spurs to me writing a poem is for me to receive one from somebody else: many of mine are written as responses to these gifts.

Although I can list these different influences and the kinds of situations in which a poem might spring forth, I cannot say that any of this really explains how a poem comes to be. There is always something mysterious, a power at work that seems quite beyond one's personal control. Actually it is being in the hands of this other power that is what I find most satisfying, not just in the writing, but in life generally. The Muse is always at work and my attitude to life is that of a spiritual artist. Art and spirituality are not, as far as I can see, two different things.

Nowadays spirituality has tended to become closely associated with morality or with certain disciplines and practices and so with a controlled approach to life, while art has largely become detached from spirituality and aesthetics is seen as a separate discipline, but I do not see things that way. Spirit is something that gets loose in the world and creates a certain amount of mischief. This is because it does create – it is creation. That is the point. It disturbs and challenges us to go beyond what we have been heretofore. Poetry disturbs, and to live a spiritual life is to feel and embody that crazy spirit that, with its irony and its sudden sprees of romp or reverie, overturns the old, yet does so in a way that still reveres and continues the thread of the past, but in an unexpected way.

David Brazier

I

Society

Her Mother's Eyes

Her mother's eyes:
of it all that is what she will never forget:
Mother's face, as she saw her there...
That is what has become engraved
on the marrow of who she is,
so much more deeply did it penetrate
than all that had gone before.

The face of a mother
who knows...
Who knows what has been done
to the daughter she bore,
who knows she has been unable to protect her own:
"If only I could have spared her that,"
they each thought, for the other.

And with the remembrance of that face
sometimes there comes
the rending, yet now fragmentary, details:
the roughness of the uniforms bruising her breasts,
the pinch pain where they gripped her,
the smell of alcohol and sweat,
the music she would never want to hear again.

She does not remember *their* eyes,
though they must have been glowing
- or were they dead? -
nor does she remember
her own impossible defence:
how her dress got torn away
nor, even, how she acquired the cuts and the burns.

Why did they not finish her
there and then
or a day or two later
with a bullet,
like they usually did?
She will never know.
A mistake perhaps.

But she rarely remembers the event itself,
now consigned to darkness,
though she always seems to carry
the sense of dirt
on the inside of her flesh,
on the soul side,
where no ordinary cleansing can erase.

No, all she remembers
is her mother's eyes.

Bosnia, 1996

Do You Have a Mother?

Do you have a mother, young man?
His mother sent him to war
to right the wrongs
his people suffered
this hundred years and more.
Her village is in the fire zone now,
no letters come any more.

Though he cries for her by night
shame keeps him mute by day
playing the part of a soldier.
He'll never murmur
"What will become of me?"
but cannot always prevent
"What has become of her?"

And even if she lives
would she recognize him now?
Would she take him back
with all he has seen,
such unmentionable things.
Could he be again
her little poppet, now?

No, the past will not come back
ever again. And tomorrow...
Better not think about tomorrow.
So, today, then:

but there is little comfort here
just a visit to the bar
and the little rooms above
where you can have a village girl
rounded up last week.

At first, seeing her
you feel nothing much...
until the flesh lays bare.
Then the compelling surge of lust,
the expanding fire of life,
comfort of contact and
oblivion of release.

Afterwards
he would cry in her arms
as if she...
Yes, as if she were his mother.
But the deed is done
and even in this half free moment
he has to pay the price
of playing the man
ready to die tomorrow.

Her village is in the fire zone now,
no letter for forty one days...
The officer says to "Get rid of the wench,"
but he lets her run off
in the morning haze.
Do you have a mother, young man?

Bosnia 1996

I Am Beirut

I am Beirut.
I am Phnom Penh, Groznyy and Kigali,
I speak a thousand languages and
my names are more than the names of God
for my children have spread across the world
to bathe in smoke at Nagasaki
and dance to trumpets that since Jericho
have crowed, since Genghis rode west
and Alexander east, and long, long before.

I am Beirut,
the pivot of the world, where continents
collide and the dust never settles
for the thought of me, a dark shadow,
hangs unspoken in every chancellery
to quicken the dead, suck pallor from the great,
and make heavy the footfalls of hope,
for I will not be silenced.

I am Beirut.
In me can you see your face
rendered gaunt, harried from the sun
into the deep recesses of hate?
It will out. How long will you ride
the fire wheel? How long repent?
Look upon me and learn, or is it too late?
You who think me far away, you too shall
know my names. I am Beirut.

We were never told

but rather our quest
began at nought then lunged further
past peace past war we warriors all longing
for glory beyond gore hot as midday
we were past night we were light
we were never told but we were sold
scolded lived in huts in palaces in
palisades where each could make his hut
pater familias shone when he chose
mother grew fecund when not shriven
a son was born after that more then more
and daughters by the score 'til we began to
ask what for for we were never told nor had
wit to read instructions in the sown-in flap
by which we fly we fall we live on scraps
salvaged by the heart from hints on wasted
afternoons when we could have been something
but all too often - all too often - because we
had never been told when we unleashed the straps
sweet sun had set and night had come upon us
all with lacerating rain of nine tails or a
thousand tails knotted for effect caught us
poor naked in our wretchedness
lunging lunging plunging
past unseen enemies impaling
ourselves on rugged ground of dreams wherein
our palaces were all turned inside out as
our warrior shout rose and rose as we composed
perfect verses of the fathers each more perfect
than that before as the rain that still tore into the
fabric of that land where we were lost caused all
to decompose for we were never told

Childhood Experience in Cyprus' Struggle for Independence

In the Austin Seven car I sat in the back seat, but always
wanted to stand even though they said it was not
safe;
Later we had to sit in an armoured personnel carrier to
take us to school: machine guns on the gates.

Mummy told me I had a good memory, but I cannot
remember what it was I had remembered on that
occasion,
But I do remember the day I found a bomb in the garden -
it looked fun, the box with plastic tubes sticking out.

Carob trees, where lizards lived, were best for climbing
because of the split down the middle of the trunk;
One day I split my head falling off a wall and another
time got a whacking bruise from swinging on a door
hook.

Those were my worst mishaps. I don't count the day I got
ambushed by a gang of Cypriot boys because
I ran fast and got away - even though I was mightily out
of breath when I got home and didn't tell Mummy
what had happened.

They put me to bed too early in the evening - I thought so
anyway - but I knew they cared which was the main
thing.
The easiest way to get to sleep was to count. There were
bombs down in the town every night - seventeen,
eighteen, nineteen.... sweet dream, night, night.

Britain and Germany

In 1902 two nations stood as one,
By links of history and culture tied;
The first had conquests second to none
And stood almighty on the tide.

The other, similarly, on land supreme
And in ingenious industry unexcelled;
Such harmony spoke like a perfect dream,
A power that could the world have quelled.

Two royal houses closely bonded,
Nations that called each other friend,
An alliance of things that corresponded,
Guarantee of peace that could not end.

A dozen years, an accident here and there,
Provocations arise: where do they come from?
Who would have thought such mutual care
Could end in the gore and mud of the Somme?

On Visiting Picardy at the Time of the Lebanon War

Sylvan soldiers stand
A poplar guard of honour
'Cross Picardy's land
Their crests bob faint bows toward
The becalmed dead 'neath their sand.
Elsewhere the world burns
With flames of hate rekindled
Across other sands
Where cedars famed of old
No longer now bear witness.

All the world's on fire
With the fire of greed, say I,
With the fire of hate.
Who will to nirvana go?
Who will bury all this woe?

The corn is golden,
The woodlands are all at peace
In Picardy now
Poplars continue to bow
To those interred at their feet.

War in the Congo

They killed the men and cooked them,
invited the women to the feast -
their women, the one's whom the dead had loved,
they tried to humiliate them like that.
You may as well kill us too,
the women said, their wound beyond bearing.

That's the way of war these days.
That's how it goes in the hidden lands
where the human animal prowls
and wonders how far he can go,
with a wound beyond bearing.

Saddam

In the land of Adam
There came a Stalin look alike in khaki,
Moustache, black, complexion, swarthy;
They called him Saddam.

He was the Tigris' iron madam;
A master of the military,
Lieutenants, in imitation, all looked as he
And, my God, he had'em.

Ruthless, he didn't give a damn
For nicety, none crossed him with impunity;
Like Hitler, he made the trains run punctually;
He was no little lamb.

All pray that one day the land that's Adam's
Will find a way less grim than Saddam's.

The Battle of Sluys 1340

At Sluys sheltered by Cadzand
The French in mighty force did stand
With allies Genoese, Spanish and Picard
Nineteen thousand stood on guard
Two hundred great galleys, frigates and more
Stood off the continental shore
Determined now to sever Edward's tie
With Flanders where his queen did lie.

Chancellor and admirals this gloomy news receiving
Advised their king: Stay home and don't be leaving.
They were sure that if sailing forth he went
They would all be dead before reaching Ghent.
Edward would have nothing of it: Cowards!
He cried. Get what ships we have: Onwards!

One hundred and thirty smaller fighting boats
Put forth from Harwich with twelve thousand men.
The enemy, in no hurry, held their stand,
Controlling the shore where England must land.
On 24th June, in the afternoon light
From the deck of the Thomas, Edward signalled the fight;
Advancing with the wind to the mouth of the Zwin,
Ship by ship by ship he would win.

As the first rank of galleys, that had been proud, shattered
Those behind, dismayed, in consternation scattered.
As the sun went down and the sea turned red
The French were seventeen thousand dead.
It was a stunning victory
Against all odds for all to see.

Sluys today is a happy town where the English and the
French
May eat chips with mayonnaise on a single tourist bench.
The battle is long forgotten; dead men speak no more;
There is peace on the golden sands of a happy tranquil
shore.
Though we can learn from heroes old
Not to be weak, but to be bold,
Let's make our boldness in peaceful cause
And put behind us all such wars.

Gun Crime

There's a lot of talk on the chattering vine
of guns and knives and youth violent crime.
"Youth," they say, "The youth of today,"
like a pestilence you don't want to stay
or commodity of plastic tat
to put away so that is that,
but blood on the streets is hot and real
from an arm or a throat that can't appeal;
did you hear a scream, a gasp or groan
that said, "in here no hope is sewn"
but only frustration at road blocked roads
where those who have nothing know they're owed
so a cut or a stab or a shot in the night
is more than just a private fight
but a cry to the court of history
on account of a stolen right to be free.

All those kids, though they're going down,
just had bad luck in choice of town,
a choice that was not theirs to make,
but they're the ones the tops forsake
to use as a scapegoat sacrifice
for shame at behaviour that "isn't nice,"
but's not so different from making war
across the seas for the sake of oil
and sending in more polished thugs
to keep the flow from coming unplugged
of liquid gold that keeps some wealthy.

The poor still lack the means to be healthy
so they fight among themselves 'til
bodies lie there dead and still,
for the real enemy's out of reach
of mind or arm - it's hide and seek.

Valentine's Day Shooting, North Illinois University

The dead are still lying;
the snow is still red;
the wheel is still turning;
the devils are fed.

Fragile beauty lies bespattered
broken on the turning wheel.
Who made the instruments of killing?
What scream impelled the knob of steel?

In my dream I see you rising,
though I know the deed is done,
yet I cry for peace and solace,
long again that we be one.

There upon the lawn, the bodies,
in the frost, like sawn off boughs,
or, in a field of new cut furrows,
worms are severed by the plough.

Ruthless is this straw dog world,
yet I was given ruth in plenty.
Oh for freedom from compassion.
Oh to be a pot that's empty.

The dead are still lying;
the blood is not cold;
our souls are on auction
- who will buy -
going... going... sold.

Fiduciary Issue

By the grace of God, queen,
Faith defender,
There it is, clear to be seen
On every piece of legal tender.

Coins today are fiduciary issue
An act of faith in themselves;
Only alloy, they could be tissue
Issued by Zurich elves.

Faith in God, faith in currency,
It's the state that puts them together;
Long believing in all three
They say we'll have sunny weather.

Coins are royalty's best adverts;
You can trust the queen in your pocket,
And trust is the only thing that averts
Mayhem and chaos: don't mock it.

Faith is the axis of all the spheres
Exploited for power and plenty,
Without it we'd all be in our biers
For our plates would all be empty.

Catching the Boat

for Binta Breeze, poet,
who immigrated to Britain as a child

Reaching out her hand
in complete submission
to the lady chosen by Grandmother
to take her on the boat
to that far away country
from which letters had come
erratically, but full of love
for eight years now
she felt within her tiny heart
the twist of anguish: for
she could no longer remember
mother's face.

Night Train in the Sugar Fields

It's cooler at night,
shunting through the cane,
what with the heat of the engine
making you sweat,
with the sun still in sight
you'd be wet through, streaming
in the steam, or midday rain,
so, here we are in the cool, dry night
cutting along on the train.

I'm sitting here thinking,
chugging through the cane,
pulling a couple of ton down the track,
enjoying the cool clout of the sea,
at least this work will
keep me from drinking:
money in the sack not the swill;
life's getting better for me,
driver of the night train.

In the Olive Shop

By the road side
amid the great flat lands,
California's central plain,
we pull in for a break.
While Greg refuels the car
we go next door
to the olive shop.

Shelf upon shelf,
so many kinds,
not to mention olive soap,
oil, essences and lotions,
plump green succulence bottled up in a hundred ways,
taste them, relish them,
buy them,
take them to the counter,
start up a casual conversation.

Notice the accent.
Italiano?
Try out a few rusty words,
have a laugh together,
think of Europe,
then discover,
he has never been there,
never felt the marble of Rome,
the glass of Milan,
steel of Umbrian heat,
silk of Mediterranean water,

never seen Naples
- cannot die yet -
grew up Italian,
at home in a land
foreign to his blood,
a bit of the melting pot
not yet melted
still yearning for
something completely unknown.

We buy the olives
and part
laughing through tears.

II

Love

Heaven Comes to Us

Love does not fly heavenward,
Heaven comes to us.
It impales itself upon my bones and yours
and stands to be stoned to death by trade
yet re-arises with an open hand,
for Love never renounces life
even when cut down by a sword,
even slain.

Love rises only as high as beings stand
for Love sees the world and is not blind,
- the only one -
for it sees futurely.
Love sustains.

Lovers live prayer and ecstasy
in this hard paradise in making
where all shall be well.

A Lover loves the sea, which he is not.
A Lover loves the land, which she is not.
Lovers love the sky, which they are not.
Lovers love each the other, whom they are not
and Lovers love those who know little of Love
for Love loves beyond itself
and rejoices.

Love never annihilates this world
but sups upon it
dining in exquisite pain,
seeing it and seeing it gone again,
- is, will be and was -
holding each specifically in a gentle hand
and dying momently from awe
upon what is to be.

Open Secret

The slender thread of life is easily broken
but this memento of my love will long betoken
the things of which we've never really spoken
and the things we've left to sleep unwoken
and though it may be we will never wake them
still in my heart I know they're not forsaken
for 'til that thread is snapped and our life taken
our love will be a secret that is open.

She Took Me

she took my bone
she took my blood
she loved and left
me where I stood
she was not bad
she was not good
she was what she was
and I understood

Rejection

His loneliness is white as the sheen on the water,
His heart is quite taken with the inn keeper's daughter;
She is the sweet delight of all the men in Kerry,
And she's such a pretty sight as makes them all be merry.
How will he win the right to be the one beside?
He asked her in the night if she would be his bride,
But she has eyes bright for another handsome lad,
She told him his lip to bite, and: Please don't be sad.

Lovers Live in a Different Land

Lovers live in a different land
They speak the language of the hand
The hand that hand in hand goes by
The hand that soothes when the eye must cry.

And it's true
That I love you
For I've seen
The grass is green

Lovers live in a different land
Where endless happiness is planned
And hands caress and never fight
But only cherish through the night.

And it's true
That I love you
For I plight
That snow is white

Lovers live in a different land
Where moonlight shines upon the sand
And as we stroll within that glow
Love's the only thing we know.

And it's true
That I love you
For as it's said
The sun is red

Lovers live in a different land
Come join me there for all we planned
Come be with me and understand
For we belong there in that land.

For it's true
That I love you
For the sky
Is ever blue

The Orange and the Rose

Orange blossom comes
while the last of last year's fruit
is still on the tree,
but the rose sheds its petals in winter
and sometimes
winter is long.

So many losses...
How can I comfort
my heart
that is torn
- not by false words -
- not by hard deeds -
by what remains
of what is gone,
by what was once here to touch
and is now disembodied
in the insanity of my brain holding on.

Many fine blossoms,
fragrant and soft hued,
have blown away
in the sharp October wind,
but even in January
there is still a hint
of orange perfume.

In spring a new rose will bloom
and she will kiss away my woe.

The Red Scarf

Pulling the red head scarf across her face,
her cheek pinked with its reflection or
the disagreement ruffling inward;
trifles stir the ashes, or the sin.

Yet still
there are birds passing
trilling to one another,
open sky or under cover.

Simple things are needed in a lover.
Things that do not exist are sweetest.
It is so hard to keep your mind
upon the horizon as you lift your
chin toward the moon. Ah, the moon!

Concealed now, the blush
of the setting sun gives promise
of peace
in the giving live long calm
pink of evening.

You turn back, a sidelong glance
past the ignition of dispute
as though unintended,
unruffled, undistended.
A moment, a look, a thing that never happened,
a simple trifle.
She ties the knot beneath her chin.

My Salt Doll Entered the Ocean

Salt doll, I can no longer sleep.
Where are you now?
I, disconsolate, sit by the tide and weep -
such pain for the loss of you;
I, a poor human;
I am not made like you.

My salt tears of grief
fall upon the rock hard shore
stranded before the ocean thief
who took you.

Baked by sun heat
each of my tears,
sad, sad, sad,
disappears
into the warmth from which I draw life,

and in the residue of my melancholy
slowly you are reforming
before me...
How many aeons 'til I see you again?

Chemistry of Mirrors

I wish he loved me as I would be loved
And thus unlock the love in me
Imprisoned as it is, not truly free,
But occasionally paroled until once more removed
Back to its cell by sudden inconsideration.
No doubt he feels the same as I,
She thought, we're not indicted by a lie,
But by symmetry of perturbation.
        Each would be cherished, each received,
        Each yearns to be noticed and not capped;
        Each longs for attention, sometimes rapt,
        Each sharply feels short change of tenderness,
        Yet each defends for fear of more distress.
We are a chemistry of mirrors, if I'm not deceived.

Coffee Shop
in San Francisco

Cafe talk - how I love it!
Between us a disc of old wood,
the worn table top,
is here and there sculpted by abrasions,
the signs of its tolerance
of our many predecessors.
What passions have danced here
over little white cream jugs?

The coffee cools between us
as woodgrain, waved like Chinese clouds,
provides motif for our
survey of one another's
swirling self-revelations.
We manoeuvre into tenderness
by tiny degrees.

No deliberate cunctation
accounts for the slippage of time
as we seek to penetrate hard knots
and trace back the rings
of our many seasons.
In the intensity of waxing intimacy
we nurture one another's
regermination.

Finally, emptying the cups of their now cold contents,
we take once more to the streets
hand in hand.

She is a House that's Empty Now

She is a house that's empty now,
curtains frayed and bedspread torn,
though I still fear her furrowed brow,
tremble and here lie forlorn.

She is a house that's full of woe,
windows broken, doors unhinged ,
the reason why I do not know,
but only that my heart was singed.

She is a garden buried deep
beneath an overgrowth of thorn
yet now I meet her in my sleep
and once again begin to mourn.

She is a road that's long and cold,
pitted now its yellow brick,
whereon my step grows slowly old,
my heart unfathomably sick.

She is a cliff that's sharp and tall
and here I stand upon the edge,
but I shall not cast off and fall,
just pass a year upon this ledge.

Perfume

I hate that the scent of your perfume
  is not meant as only for me
for my soul is aflame with your love light,
  your wisp of sweet mystery,
now the stars seem alone in their sparkle,
  their darts are not passing me by,
for the hemlock of grief mounts so slowly
  and my old life is waiting to die.

Though to love and to lose is as common
  as the rain in the afternoon
how you came, how you went, how we struggled,
  how our doom came a lifetime too soon,
leaves me tossed like soft foam on the ocean
  that is raised and then blown away;
leaves me wretched and ragged and dream-wrecked
  in the pink of the break of the day.

I hate that the scent of your perfume
  is not meant as only for me
for I'm jealous and angry and wounded
  and all that I'm not s'posed to be
and my healing is still in the far off,
  on the shore of another far land,
like the shore where we stood when we promised
  and your scent made me understand.

Yes, to love and to lose is as common
  as the rain in the afternoon
that washes away all the vows
  that were born 'neath the changeable moon
and one day I'll rise up from my ashes,
  and be stronger and wiser for sure
but for now I'll remember the perfume
  and dream for a month or two more.

A Pair of Pots

His life was potter's earth upon her wheel
and she the glaze upon his earthenware
and they were fired together in the kiln
of love that burnt away all trace of care

for he was turned from dust of Kao-lin Shan,
she the finer ore that turned him coy,
so they, a precious porcelain from clay,
were hearts translucent, vitrified in joy.

For Richard

Come, come, arrive,
it won't be long, we're not too old,
we need not strive when we have song.
When we have verses made from silver
tripping from a brim full pitcher
over-flowing gems cascading
will you be my harvester?
Will you catch those falling tresses
tumbling down from angel dresses
freeing beauty from the witch's
curse of jealousy and loss?
You shall be my friend eternal,
we shall fly across horizons,
over tunnels, under ditches,
through a sky all made of moss,
beyond the knowledge of the living
into lands of gold.

Friendship

My match blew out suddenly
in the gust of your love;
my burnt fingers smarting
my nostrils still sulphur
my eyes strangely dazzled
the darkness a softness
your velvet illumined
by echoes of gleaming
like fireflies mingling
snatching the moment
before parting in silence
before knowing the friendship
that caught me in earnest
was you.

Catering Trade Flirtation

Poetta. Operetta. Borboleta. Nothing terse.
Immersed à deux, Rebecca
gossips in the café kitchen
as Ahmed, workmate,
in precocious domesticity,
chops;
she 17, he one year older.
Only two on duty today.

Commerce of vernacular verse
runs brown and hot;
drink it up. His sparser banter
counter-points her rough silver: a gentle game of tag.
Now there'll be no way, calm or heady, to forget her.

Chocolate steams in shapely cups. Customers
come and go lifting the trance - or curse -
only for moments as indecision hovers over the counter.

One day they'll kiss, but for now
trade verses - his mostly gesture.
She: "Shall we fry together?"

Fragility

White chrysanthemums
offset the dark sky above
yet in his fond dream
it had been her spread white frock
beneath a sky of azure.

He picked one sweet bloom
and held its fragility
whispering her name
as if to conjure the dead
for she knows him now no more.

III
Philosophy

From a Small Angel

Little light, who is your sister, where does she live?
I ask, wonderingly, yet not quite fully concentrating.
She lives on the ring finger of God. I am her twin.
Wonder is my name. She speaks gaily.
There seemed nothing more to say, but
more attentive now, I would have liked to know them further.

Little light, who is your brother, what about him?
You ask too much. You must also look and learn
not merely ask of me, says she, without a trace of malice,
and rebuked, but glad, I feel the truth of it.

Little light, then show me how to learn, for
I am only dark, with no sweet-light of my own.
Just continue to say so, she said, for saying so is seeking well.
On your jet core dance all the lights you need know.
And then she was gone.

What Did You Do In History?

What did you do in history?
Were you a conquistador,
an angry painter, a gentle saint?
Did you make love or war?

Who are the ones you cared to see?
Where now the off-spring you bore?
What did you do in history?
Rich man, pauper or whore?

Was it touch or tone that roused you?
Were you fine and bold or faint?
Did you live in the light fate gave you?
Do you still have the age old taint?

Is it pillage and rape that attracts you?
Can the karma ever come loose?
I have heard it said, "To yourself be true,"
But what if your self was a goose?

A rebel on canvas - a genius, maybe,
or just a philandering bore,
unwittingly playing to a mystery -
an old love in an older war.

Whence comes the grace to set us free
from our hard, old, heartwood core?
What will we be in history?
What were we sent here for?

Many Gods

Each has his God, be it evolution,
money, love, light, totem or revolution.
Each has his bane to be voted out,
favourite iniquity - whispered sin or tawdry shout.
Each has her God, favoured solution,
cure for all ills, world's needed ablution.
Each has her hate to abuse and malign,
the low ground to finger with contemptuous sign.

We are partial, not dispassionate much,
each has dogmas to which to clutch,
rarely thought through, never reconciled
with logic enough to content a child.

Whether it's science or creed you rely on
be sure each strives to reach his Zion.

Life Journey

Did she live before she died?
Did she die before she cried?
Did she grow before she lied?
Did she love before she sighed?

She believed before she hoped.
She received before she coped.
She gave all before she moped.
She deceived and then eloped.

She grew up beyond ideals;
found she was the one who steals,
found the gift that then reveals
the secret that one then conceals.

Unto the end and everlasting
lived a story free of fasting
like a fisherman who's casting
for a longing soul that's gasping.

Did she use up every talent?
Did she feel her heart relent?
Did she abandon what she lent?
Did she relish what she spent?

She found to build is to destroy.
She found that life is not a toy.
She found the anchor of her buoy.
She found one thing that does not cloy.

War War

War, war, where will we be without it?
What will we do to flout it?
What else can clean our slate,
make it stop, make it wait,
make it pause its unrelenting toil
that coils us in its sang and maw?
When will our peace be such a peace
as not to end in war?
When will we know what we are for?
What all this world and woe and wall
and stop and go,
goodbye, hello,
and more and more and more are for?
When will we see what Buddha saw,
what Jesus bore
what's Allah's law?
What merciful, compassionate,
can be the very end of that,
the omega and alpha too
without the strife of me and you
like thunder clouds of fate.
When is it we'll be true?

Devil's Kitchen

The devil's in his kitchen,
making up the broth
for angels in the dining hall,
who think it comes from God.
The back door's swinging open
to admit a new recruit -
set him to work on chopping
'til his arms are falling off.
We're not here to slack, you know.
I hate that holy lute.
They've been playing hymns all morning.
They can't bear to hear us scoff,
but there's no conversion in us,
we who slave behind the shop,
while they sit around and gossip
as though time will never stop
with their condescending manners
and their supping on the cream
as though all that to them matters
is fulfilment of *their* dream,
but their time in heaven lessens
with the ticking and the chimes
and one day they'll be in here for
a bit of working time.

Here in the devil's kitchen
where our fallen angels slave
one learns the real meaning of
a life beyond the grave
for there's nothing worse than heaven
out there in the restaurant
where they depend on us lot
for their roasting and their fries
but they never know reality
- that burns in devil eyes.
So down here in the galley
you can skivvy all day through
and you know the score and know the lash
and know the very truth,
but the swooners at the tables
who are downing double luxe
live blindly on their laurels
till they drown in their gold cups.

Liberation

Life is a love letter written on sand
sand that is diamond that lights up my hand
hands that caress what is tender or torn
’til the tearing is caught on a barb or a thorn
and the thorns that he wore are crushed under the tide
of the crashing and rushing spring surge we can’t hide
but can only remember with aching and hope
reminiscing on times when we planned to elope
but were caught and held under by touching mementoes
of times when we had many friends and no real foes
but only a womb that was bitter and sweet
that held us and told us that all was complete
’til the envelope opened and now we are out
with a letter to read to say what it's about
for this hand is for you and this hand is for peace
as the signature written says merely "Release".

Compostello

A longing calls me westward along the pilgrim trail;
a pilgrim hood I'll have and a staff and donkey friend,
a metal cup to scoop spring water for sweet ale
and strong boots for walking to the end.

Toward the setting sun, with hope upon my heart,
I'll stroll into vermilion against a sky of limpid blue;
as the pale moon cares for the region I depart
wayside forget-me-nots will keep me true.

It is an angel takes me there, she of the evening tide,
when work is done, heart is free, I hear her call
and dreams come of waltzing, donkey at my side,
as we've dreamt since we first did fall.

A Secret Line of Pearls

The irony of history is Allah's they say,
For He, by right, is king of night and of day.

When we look back and see the path we've
wended
We know by Allah we were unknowingly
befriended.

A line we see direct from A to B to C, no
deviation;
Though at the time it seemed diverse
peregrination.

Intending a certain goal, as we thought, we set
out in care
And by mishap, mischance, misadventure,
arrived elsewhere.

We arrived exactly where He'd have us be and
know our state,
Near to the merciful, the compassionate, along
a line that's straight.

Vulture Peak

The bodhisattvas came to Vulture Peak
Enlightenment for all the world to seek
They found the one who showed the light and truth did speak
Completely perfect Buddha
Om, Ah, Hum

They bowed and asked the Holy One to teach
What must be done by one who peace would reach
With bated breath they waited then to hear his speech
Completely perfect Buddha
Om, Ah, Hum

He saw their hearts were full of silent zest
His smile was warm as he praised their request
He is the one who can release all of us best
Completely perfect Buddha
Om, Ah, Hum

He taught the way to act from emptiness
He taught the way to end the world's distress
His Dharma seal he will upon our hearts impress
Completely perfect Buddha
Om, Ah, Hum

Although we bleed he will our hearts all mend
His blessings unto all creatures he'll send
We turn our hearts to him and find a perfect friend
Completely perfect Buddha
Om, Ah, Hum

Angel Wings

A soul may rise on butterfly wings;
they should be enough,
after all, a soul is not supposed to weigh much
and butterflies don't eat a lot nor live long,
but maybe even that kiss of mortality
would prove too much.

Can the soul bear to wear
an exoskeleton of grist, even one so small?
How does it bear *us*, one wonders.

Souls are supposed to be innocent creatures -
much more so than butterflies, anyway,
whose sole purpose is to get it off
and get some eggs deposited quickly
before the weather changes. Are
souls like that, do you think? Do they
come here with a grubby mission
to deposit a bit of slime somewhere
where it will have a good supply of cabbage to eat?

I'll ask an angel. There's one hereabouts
collecting wing dust from dead butterflies -
I'm sure he'll know.

Heavenly Light
(after reading Pessoa)

A dwarf may have a rainbow for a soul,
purple and shocking marine,
ultra pink, and pomegranate green
and stride with strides than you have ever seen
as steaming life ever fills a furnace with hot coal.

A tall man may be shortened, a broken pole,
nursing thoughts trivial and mean
under a bushel, unseen,
on unlived life, the accusing might-have-been,
the shriven liver that none think ever to console.

The ledger may be larger than one's heart,
the shadow of a judgement,
the echoes of a long lament,
the harm done, the broken vase, the injury unmeant,
the cruel decree by which the unclean leper must depart.

Each morning turn the key, descend the step, time to start,
arrive at a dull table,
perform as you are able,
do your hired duty 'til you're sent back to your stable,
never ask the moral, pass your day remote from art.

Pedestrian bones, worn neurons, can they still dance?
A wick lost in wax can be trimmed;
a flame can rise undimmed.
See the broken man - the lamp lighter comes for him
and from that deposit in heaven now there'll be a small
advance.

Lineage

The line that someone else took
you cannot follow,
for even with perfect choreography
you are not he
and the geography of his moments
has already eroded
into a now past age.

The line that someone else took
lies like a tempting word
in a golden book,
a book that never lies;
yet you can never make *that* word
your own.

The line that someone else took
is a line upon the waters
made by the under tow
that startled him and made him go
where
you cannot follow.

The line that someone else took
is now a line in the heaven
of a different age
to inspire the knights
of tomorrow.

The line that you take
will join invisible dots
not already connected
for you have a further part
in the great design
of the age of tomorrow.

Your line is not that old line,
but as an inspired knight
crossing the desert of your indiscretions
you will see the waters newly part
and led by your much bruised heart
you will follow.

Ralph

When Ralph committed suicide
and used a knife to do it
we realised, for the first time,
mentally going through it,
that he had actually existed.
- No, really lived, like you and I do,
not merely stubbornly persisted
in being there -
that, everyone knew,
but was quickened with a suffering soul
that could have been cared about
with enough going on to cut his own carcass
and let that soul out
and just for once be seen.

It's shocking really -
that others do exist, I mean.
Day to day one doesn't take it seriously,
lip service, of course,
but to feel it, know it, inside,
gives one pause.
Is it just propriety
that wants to intervene,
that dwells upon
the way it could have been?
A knife, of all things,
is somehow so crude,
how could one always inoffensive
have suddenly been so rude?

I Prefer the Old Gods

I prefer the old gods,
the ones who fuck
and know what spite feels like,
the ones who fight against the odds
and chance their luck
and throw their fallen rival in a dyke.
Those gods are more real
than the effete goodness praised today:
no thorn, no brier, just limpid petal!
Gods who can steal:
to them - yes, they - you can pray
standing up, in the fullness of your mettle.

Time

At this juncture there is time
time to be ahead of time or fall behind
occasion to be obsolete or *à la mode*
time to spend or time to save
but only for the time being
only in the good times can we afford to kill time
and still be in time enough to have time to spare
for there's been many times when merely shilly-shallying
has let the bad times in and then we've not had time
to pass the time of day.

IV

Who Am I?

Many Draughts of Life I Took

Many draughts of life I took
and many were the guises
by which I sampled from its hook
and thwarted its assizes.

There's always last a price to pay
said bosses, friends and scholars,
but I always got away
with less than pounds or dollars.

The cost is not in property,
but the being of the owner.
So stow your soul, live prettily,
and you'll not need disown her.

Then when you're weighed the dust falls by
like water in a basket -
they cannot trap a laugh or sigh
within a metal casket.

Just pay and give them all you are
and there'll be twice tomorrow
for when you're guided by a star
you never need to borrow.

Pick fragrant blooms that don't resist:
for each I'll give you seven;
for all the flowers you have kissed
are blooming now in heaven.

When I Go to Heaven

When I go to heaven
I shall have time
to read dictionaries.
My twenty volume set
shall be bound with red covers
and embossed with gold type
on the front and spine,
solid to the hands
but not so heavy
as to tire the elbows.
Inside will be
the etymology
of all the tongues of Earth
showing their family
relations to one another.
In the morning
I shall read the twenty volumes
as a liturgy
and in the afternoon
I shall write verse.

The Lists

Dick the Bad - I knew his dates. On Tuesdays we
had double lessons in the impenetrable afternoon.
I loaned Mary my pen, hopefully.

We were god kings then; Tiu and Woden, Gleipnir
and Sleipnir, sallying over floods into clefts of the
imagination; doubly restored after fatal encounters.

Soar heart! Valhalla? A return please. Or Hades.
Sticks mark the border. Password or coin? Once it
is paid, will there be a homeward track in the maze?

Her shade darkened the passage: a hint of something
serious. The knell brought us back to history and
homework. Notes passed under desks.

He was the last one smitten in battle, but I
was young and just venturing in the lists.

Irene

When I was young she taught me rhymes to say:
the poet celebrates by night
the irony of day;
for though so many years are passed and gone into the dream
they are so many entries in
my journal of Irene.

Death Missed Me

Somehow death missed me again today.
He just keeps on standing me up.
Just when I think we are going to play
He moves and capsizes my cup.

It was the draught I got from a Greek:
To know yourself and be damned;
But while I'm playing this hide and seek
My in-tray is getting spammed.

The hemlock is cooling and I'm getting stale
While the god in me's feeling the pain.
What they said was heaven is really a gaol
But it won't stop me coming again.

If he comes round tomorrow, just tell him I'm out
And to pick up the tab on the sill;
If it isn't enough, there's some contraband stuff,
Which should be enough for the bill.

Somehow death missed me again today,
His eye was just not on the ball,
So I'll hang out my heart with a word and a laugh
'Til I hear his final call.

Not Selected

If life was a choir I'd not have been selected
but in cacophony I have my place
at least until I come up face to face
with those who think we should have been inspected
and checked for all our previous undetected
errors, omissions, torts, wasted space
and other forms of error and disgrace
that narrow minds delight to have dissected.

If life was a choir I'd never ring a bell
or sing a song in hope of getting fed
for with no possibility of hell
where prayers and only pious words are said
there is no need for anyone to spell
out mantras for the living or the dead.

Travelling Friend

Tom knew me since the world began:
with restless spirit he theorised,
avoided work, womanised,
catch as catch can;
he was a travelling man,
liked to indulge, oversized,
obsessive, mesmerised,
couldn't settle, tried to get even.
He was not one to rely upon
- now you see him, now he's gone -
but a jovial friend
who'd come and go
telling his tale - the joy, the woe -
and I found my own way to correspond
with the world's most dapper vagabond.

Our Big Blue Camper Van

How we loved you, our blue snail shell
wherein we cuddled on a dark night
after parking discreetly without legal right
in the woods and slept 'til the knell
of church bells told of dawn. How
we nurtured you over high passes and
down again to Mediterranean sand.
Yes, you were our magic ship, our prow
that sped us into adventure near and far;
and how sorely we lament the day
you died after long ailment and decline;
I cannot think of you but pine
for those honey days long gone, far away.
You were so much more fun....
                                        than a car.

Dedicate a Wooden Bench

When I die
dedicate a wooden bench,
put it in the arboretum,
or the sea front at Ilfracombe
amidst the stunted palms and faint aromas
of mixed pollen, where old people
walk, totter or sit
as I do.

All my life I've been
too old and too young.

"In memory of Percy Huxtable
from his loving wife and daughter
1926 to 1997"
I wonder about you, Percy,
as I sit on your brown, sturdy planks
overlooking the town.
Never knew you, as far as I know;
but what of those who grieve,
as I do?

The gulls are eternal,
in their forlorn joy,
prowess on wing, they sing
of cliffs and nests, mates and storms.

March sunshine is weak as
the muffled pensioner making her way
down the hill, swaddled
in jumpers and anonymity.
How much longer will those wizened muscles
brave this gradient?
Does she have a spouse and daughter
to dedicate a bench?
I guess not.

People pass and I guess, but what do I know?
A woman parking a car catches my eye
to tell me that "They are fools,"
something about changing prices.
Ah, that's what matters after all,
prices and propriety,
don't go neglecting them,
as I do.

I'll just sit here and weep a bit
and think of Dad in his South Devon grave.
Do they remember him at the church,
atheist that he was?
Perhaps I'll dedicate a seat
on a hill above Torquay.

Until You've Done it

Divorce is unthinkable, until you've done it,
but after passing through the invisible wall
one may emerge strangely purified of conceit
as if following what one thought a devil's call
one encountered an angel, and falling at its feet
realized that all this time one had been in thrall
to a social dogma that could only mean defeat -
struggling not to grow up, or stand at all,
but remain infantile, prematurely and falsely complete.

V
Nature

Evening

From my chair at the window the middle distant yet imposing Cypress shape stands densely keen, sharply chiselled, darker than graphite. The sky behind is still discernibly blue with three brush strokes of paler rag torn cloud. Nearer objects, the fir in our garden, the neighbour's house, are already almost completely black, simple masses adding bulk, but the annexe roof still has a regular patterning of ashen flecks delineating tile.

The primal condition of things: imperceptible fading before the gaze that steadily loses its grasp; irresistible, melting to invisibility, yet, before departure most stark, more acute than in full light.

Now the dark is completing its saturation. Only two elements remain having devoured all further detail as though it never were: black mass below and over it a darkening, more opaque than slate, that yet, even now, retains the faintest hint of blue.

Time to shut the curtains and end my observation of the darkening hour. Even as I think it the two begriming zones are shedding their distinction. Amorphic finality consumes all. I too am merged into obscurity in which the tiredness of my mind cannot be set apart from the muddied turmoil of a day full as the garden with its now invisible plants.

Danny the Fox

Old Danny, the fox, has a glint in his eye,
out hunting for a hen,
he’s done his run along the fence, past sty
and up the fen,
with a touch of guile he’ll see you by;
you’ll never suspect his den;

but, of a morning, if you're sprightly in the gloom
or out without your dog
you may spot the glitter of his eye
as he goes past the log
across the stream and through the fence
and you may count upon it
that before you get back to your fire
old Danny's said his sonnet,
been through the coop and up the hill
and cut back through the stable
and there’s a bird laid for the cubs
upon the vulpes’ table.

Mule Pedigree

A mule of equine ancestry
must know he has another part
the chevaline and haughty look
conceals a docile donkey heart

and no one would be divident
without dubitancy or pause
nor see the parts asunder rent
nor only catch the whiff of horse

for donkey is not just an ass
but also India's kiang
deriving from the highest caste
of onager from Turkestan.

Starling

Starlings are darlings, fallings from heaven,
jewel bags of blackness, breasts full of leaven,
shining and asking, dining and basking,
sweet living black things with eyes of jet silver,
replete strutting chic wings that leave nothing over:
they copy the cries of the garden lawn mower,
the rasp of the scythe, the song of the sower;
they are not a soft dove, nor yet a rag robin,
not quite a crow, love, nor yet a pied bobbin,
but they are full something with pride more than plover,
so of all the bird kind take starling and love her.

Daffs

Alongside the path the daffodils
are bent, scattered, windswept, yet
these dauntless princes of spring, non-violent
soldiers in the army of courtesy
that ravishes old mistress Winter one last time
stirring up her hail and wrath
rave on. Our path
decked with them entices the more
for their battered appearance.
We come back clutching the wounded,
offer them in vases for the delight
of those less keen to venture.

Pause on the Footpath into Leicester

From opposite the gasometer on a towpath bench,
choosing carefully so as not to sit in detritus,
I watch coots go round the bulrush bed.

The water reflects yellow from coiled tubes
in the works between bank and tank.
Reflections of three trees slice the surface
upstream of the coils, while small clouds
lounge at my feet.

Upstream further it's all green
or more like khaki with mallards merging in.

Passers-by keep up a brisk pace
as it's a mile to anywhere from here.

VI
What Is Poetry?

Sharper Lines

The ancients scanned their lovers from afar
so could pen stanzas as unalloyed rods
of light, delight, and charm, enthused as from the gods.

We moderns inhabit the cheap stalls, brash as we are,
hungry for detailed close-ups, so our star
has little opportunity for art. We hear the cues
for dropped lines and get less flattering views.

Therefore our verse, written from just below the bar,
has a keener, acerbic quality by far.

Summer day comparisons may still hold
if, versifier, you are old or bold,
but contemporary poets are less fair, and do so tar
their ladies as would astonish those earlier men.
Yes, today's keyboard is much sharper than their pen.

Say Now

What's a poet? What's a pound?
Can we weigh it? Is it round?
Am I a poem, or just a ditty?
Am I a play, or just a pity?
Where do ideas spend their days
before they fall into my haze
and play?

Can I be invisible to poetry?

Can my hand write not knowing who the next
word is going to be or who its mother is or know
if she is crying for it to come back after its late
meander wandering wantonly into my verse
so far into the evening past the ebony pool
with all its fast fading reflections singing tenderly
to one another in ever finer silk tones as
the great conductor goes slowly retiring in the west
behind the blank hills that dominate jaggedly
beyond the lateral road where blackness
as of deep water consumes the breath of God
until there is again something upon the deep
some word waiting to be rekindled
waiting to catch the dropped stitch
by which worlds are born and the way home lost?

Written 25 March 2008
slightly modified from the version published in Stanza (37, summer 2008)

The Notes will Play Themselves

I played a single note.
It could not live alone.
It played upon a blue green hill
where goat leaf vines were sown.
It found six playmates on the hill
amidst the tinkling bells -
a pastoral sound, a symphony,
coloured as the Book of Kells.
It danced and jingled down a brook
and gathered wild wild seeds;
it sang the song of a sweet girl's look
as she threaded acorn beads.
The notes went on and played themselves
and lay me on the loam
to find a bride among the elves
and a leaf to float me home.

Other Colours

There will be other colours
They will be rough and hot
Or they will fall metallic on
The stone stepping clatter
From the cellar
Of your dreams.

There will be vermilion
Curves and crescents
Severed
To express the pus
From the boils
Of your screams.

There, yes, there!
Don't you see them on the hills
In the corners
And the shadows of
Sheets soiled by
The amour of disgrace?

Don't you hear the crashing
Gnashing on the anvil
That's no mask
But just the pallor
Of your ripped off face?

There will be other colours
Not just blood
And not just blushes
But the flush of nails
Dancing on the crosses
Of your gains.

For a poem's not just water
Softly dripping
But the dripping
Of your fat
From the entrails of your pains.

Yes, there'll be other colours
In the pot.

Tree Observed from a Gate

Aspic matrix of overlapping twigs
gaunt sticks of oak in December's defoliation
posture against grey abstraction
that endlessly stirs.

The poem of it awakes flesh and eye,
no words as such,
but somehow the mould was there:
clauses could be cast if one had time and will for it.

Pour the molten grammar out
into those twigs to make linear stays
for stanzas,

but this is not a mould to break:
the poem is not in the words or even the wood - they decorate;
the poem is in the hint of eternity
elusive among those dark inchoate spikes.

To S.T.Coleridge

When I reflect on my strange symmetry,
The pious and profane in equal parts,
The balance of my soul that sets me free,
The poetic turn with which my rapture starts;
When I propose or compose some bright thing,
Dear to my heart as dearer still to thine,
The jewels and mystic ointment of a king,
The pearl from wisdom's oracle divine;
Then do I recall and hope I'm not mistaken,
Your gracious work of sweetness and your
        power,
Amidst all wild thought, mesmeric or misshapen,
Against all fantastic ogres of the hour;
When I reflect on this strange symmetry
I see I owe a boundless debt to thee.

Modern Poetry

Poetry is just what's fashion, they say,
what's in, what's out, what's not cliché:
No Capital Letters, don't make it rhyme -
Wordsworth wouldn't get published today.

Minimalism's become the norm,
and don't end a line with "and",
be "kitchen sink", no editor can stand
a work in classic standard form.

Rare things and common interpose,
make it look a bit like prose.
If you need a form, I would incline
to the sonnet with an extra line
on a theme of eating chips in hell
with the tenderness of a villanelle;
but, trust the Muse - you never can tell.

Poet's Complaint at Being Woken from Sleep by a Verse Insistent to be Written

Why did you wake me, and so sharply, then?
When I might have rested in the early hours,
you took advantage of my weakened powers,
insistent that I take again my pen?

Why, when I thought that I had shut you out,
or rather that you'd kindly left and gone
to wander elsewhere and let me carry on
alone, free from your stick, your prod and clout?

Have I not written enough for you, Muse,
must I slave forever in your manufactory,
scribbler of verses clear, cunning or refractory,
fictions, facts or fancies that confuse?

You are a devil in my brain -
I see you've had your way with me again.

VII
Nonsense

Poetry does not have to make sense – well, not ordinary sense, anyway. Many great poets wrote nonsense verse. Sometimes, of course, there are truths hidden beneath the surface. Gayomart, by the way, was another name for Adam, the first human being.

Yak Yak

Once a yak making cheese;
once a buddha on a breeze;
once a gunman toting lead;
once a pro upon a bed;
once a priestly man with beads;
once a parrot eating seeds;
once alive, but sometimes dead;
once a heart that had no head;
once a tongue just saying verse;
once a sinner, once much worse.

Riding on the yak he went
to the heaven Buddha sent,
took the gunmen and the pros
a-dancing at Geronimo's.
They ate the seeds, the heart and brains,
the tongue they left to pay for pains.
The sinner said a final curse
before they left to catch the hearse.

Was it Gayomart?

Was it Gayomart who got us all gavotting
on the garish Gaulish mountains
or a Gaussian fluctuation
in the Massif orchestrated by Massine?

And did our gay gavotting
reach the Meuse or Bar-le-Duc
or merely leave us
mewling melancholy in the mews?

I like those shoes.
Where did you get them darling?
Was it for a carioca
or a samba in Savona?

I wish I'd known you sooner,
such a crooner for the moon
in the bawdy afternoon.

Though Selene hides coyly swooning in the clouds
our Endymion
gets distracted by her silver:
the gaudy, Guatamalan guava
is better than a grump.

Yes, was it Gayomart
or just a frump?

Tinker's Visit

When the tinker comes a knocking
and the cullis guard is tired of his duty
Mary puts her apples in her stocking
and contemplates her scuttle and its beauty
for eating double dinners is quite sexy
but the ostrich has no way of slicing cheese
especially when the edges are so waxy
and the tailor is reclining at his ease
on the sofa with the muslin dappled edges
that she sewed there on a winter afternoon
when the swans had tired of eating orange sedges
and the gardener had pruned the last balloon.
So I can't say why he came there in his socks
or ate the juicy apple in its nest
but we knew he was as cunning as a fox
so we thought that silence suited him the best.